Life in a Cave

First published in the United Kingdom in 2007 by
Sutton Publishing, an imprint of NPI Media Group
Limited · Cirencester Road · Chalford · Stroud ·
Gloucestershire · GL6 8PE

British Library Cataloguing in Publication Data
A catalogue record for this book is available from the
British Library.

ISBN 978 0 7509 4641 4

Typesetting and origination by
NPI Media Group Limited.
Printed and bound in England.

Life in a Cave

PAUL JORDAN

SUTTON PUBLISHING

Contents

1   People and Caves   7

2   Early Man   15

3   The Neanderthal Era   30

4   The Ice Age World   48

5   Upper Palaeolithic Life in Caves   73

CHAPTER 1

People and Caves

Our earliest ancestors in Africa did not live in caves: they lived in the trees. Later they ventured onto the savannah and were able to spread around the tropical and subtropical world, even when the era of the ice ages was coming on, without needing the shelter of caves. Only in the cold environments of the northern latitudes in the times of full glaciation did people develop the way of life we can reconstruct for our 'caveman' forebears. Even then, they by no means in all times and places lived in caves.

This book tells the story of the lives of our fully human ancestors (*Homo sapiens sapiens*) and their close relatives the Neanderthalers (*Homo sapiens neanderthalensis*) who lived in Europe and Western Asia, often in caves, during the last ice age. (That epoch ended about 10,000 years ago - before the invention of farming, urban living, writing, the wheel, and so much else we regard as natural to our lives.) Of course, for the 'caveman' way of life to have ever come about, there needed to be both human evolution and the formation of caves.

Caves and cave systems come into being as the result of natural processes and natural processes destroy them in the end: few caves are very old in geological terms, often younger in fact than the oldest fossils of our ancestors. Caves come in a variety of shapes and sizes because they are formed by different processes acting on different rocks and we know them at different stages of their creation and destruction. Some of the caves we know – and there must be many we do not – have been found in the course of mining operations. But most caves are evident to us, as they were to our ancestors, because they have visible openings. Some caves present themselves as a single, large and open cavern or little more than an overhanging shelter, while others form part of deep underground systems with negotiable passages including pits and chimneys or with quite impassable crawlways. In the depths of such systems there may be water in the form of streams, lakes and waterfalls and a myriad of exotic cave deposits including crystals and stalactites and stalagmites. The large open caves and rock overhangs offer people shelter from enemies and the elements, while the deep systems offer extraordinary experiences and mysteries. Our ancestors explored both situations.

Landscapes endowed with limestone cave systems are called 'karsts' and a world map of such landscapes shows the area around the Mediterranean and up into temperate northern Europe well pocked with such features. The same is true across the Middle East to the Far East, down East Africa to the south-west of the African continent, over Australasia and especially in southern Australia. Caves are found across the USA and down into Central America along with western South America. There are also stray pepperings into Scandinavia and across Russia and Siberia. It is especially the northern and eastern Mediterranean regions, together with Europe from northern Spain across to Russia, that set the stage for the story of prehistoric human life in the last ice age.

How Caves Begin and End

Rocks like limestone are soluble in water and the caves that form in them are called solution caves. Europe has some very impressive solution caves – in Belgium, France and Spain and eastwards in the Alps to the Adriatic. There are processes other than solution that can create caves, or at least start them off, but most caves have been largely 'excavated' by running water, not so much in the way that a river scours its course but rather by the sheer dissolving effect (solution) of running, circulating, percolating water.

Some caves were started when cavities were left in the layer formations of marine deposits (or in lava flows). The sea has played a big part in the making of coastal caves as a result of sea-driven erosion with sand and pebbles and boulders, or just pressure of the waves aided by chemical action or the boring of marine organisms. Bodies of water have also played a part in the generation of caves along stream banks and lake margins. Sometimes weather alone can eat out caves in the weaker members of rock structures with the action of rain, wind-driven sand and regular alternations of frost and thaw or wetting and drying. Even rock-splitting plants can initiate the process of cave making, but solution remains the chief cause of most caves, including the most complex and spectacular, whether working on cavities already available or creating its own from scratch. Plain water is enough – its natural acids do the dissolving as it soaks into the terrain and finds its way through the weaknesses in the rock. Of course, it has plenty of time to work in, by our standards, and there are many variables in the process of cave formation: of temperature, pressure, chemical concentrations, rate of refreshment with more water, to say nothing of the nature of the rock involved.

In the formation of cave systems, a complex pattern develops – of run-off variations, stream diversions, free discharges and blockages, of deepening runs of underground water along lines of joints and faults in the rock, of collapses above and below ground. By such means were the very varied cave systems of the world created: by such means, too, are cave systems eventually destroyed, with the occasional help of other factors like earthquakes and all against the background of the world's dynamic weather systems and ever-changing climate. Some caves just get silted up or blocked with larger rubble. Rock falls, whether due simply to ongoing solution or to seismic shocks, can be the beginning of the end for caves, as further solution works on the rubble and weather erosion enters the picture. While they last, caves can be subject to quite startling changes of circumstance: geological upheaval can place sea caves high above the waters that initiated them, while rising sea levels in the warm, melting times between ice ages can bring the sea to their door, so to speak.

Caves for People

The characteristic cave of what we may think of as the 'caveman' era, handily overlooking a watercourse with plenty of game passing by, comes about when the stream's erosion of its course exposes caves along its banks and goes on to cut its way down below them. There are caves just like that, notably in the Périgord region of France where so much important evidence of our relatively recent Neanderthal cousins and Crô-

Magnon ancestors has come to light in the valleys of rivers
like the Dordogne. But most of the very earliest human
remains – the bones of the people and the stone tools
they made – have not come from caves. This is partly
because some of the caves they may have used have
not survived to our day and their contents are lost. It
is also because caves were not the only or even the
main places where very early people lived and laboured.
Caves were never available (or required) in some of
the regions occupied by evolving humanity and even
where they were occupied there was still a need for
open-air camps and work sites. The archaeological
remains of these open-air sites are harder to find than
those from caves, in which materials can survive in
much better shape and order, with layers of stratigraphy
to help date them. Stone tools transported and rolled
in old river gravels (their makers were working on the
welcoming banks of long lost or wandered streams) are
all we have to chart some epochs of human evolution.
In some places, like Eastern Europe which does on
occasion afford us some magnificent open-air sites, the
advance and retreat of the ice ages' glaciers and their
floodwater run-offs have erased a great deal of evidence

for the highly significant open-air aspect of 'caveman' times. But its significance must be remembered, along perhaps with an appeal for the abolition of this 'caveman' notion altogether, not least in view of its lingering sexist connotations. The people whose lives we shall be considering belonged to the Old Stone Age, before the development of polished stone implements let alone of metal ones, though they employed wood and sometimes bone and antler too: archaeologists call them palaeolithic people and we can now fix our sights on their appearance in the archaeological record after millions of years of evolution in Africa.

CHAPTER 2

Early Man

Humanity has evolved against a backdrop of climatic change: whatever the future holds it is fair to say that the past 7 million years or so, during which time we parted evolutionary company with our closest relatives the chimpanzees, have been coldish and sometimes very cold times. There have been warmer fluctuations during this period, but the world was once very much more dependably warm with little difference in warmth between the poles and the equator: after very dim and distant ice ages of the remote past, these generally very warm conditions went on and on until about 55 million years ago (mya). Thereafter there was a slow decline in world temperatures reaching a low (though not as low as today) between 35 and 25 mya. The factors that interact to change the earth's temperatures include the heat output of the sun, the degree of transparency of the earth's atmosphere (influenced, for example, by volcanic eruptions or degree of cloud formation) and the variability of the shape of our planet's orbit around the sun and of its axis of spin relative to orbit; of course, we have been busy adding a human factor to this picture of late.

The Primates, the order of mammals to which we belong, begin to emerge in the fossil record a little before 55 mya, evolving out of small fruit - and insect - eating animals. By 55 mya, the distinctive Primate trait of large brain for body size is evident – the brain capacity partly evolved to handle high quality vision to help with the identification of good ripe fruit and fresh leaves against the clutter of the dark forest in which these creatures lived. Large brains also help with complex social relations, which was to be very important as the human line evolved.

By the time of that long cooler spell between 35 and 25 mya the Primates had greatly diversified, with the presence of monkey-like creatures at the start of this time span and ape-like ones too at the end. A peak of warming occurred thereafter, at around 16 mya, but it was followed by a series of drops in temperature at about 12, 10 and 7 mya, ushering in the long epoch of fluctuating ice ages and 'interglacials' during which human evolution has taken place and in which we still live, with permanent ice in Antarctica. While the high latitudes got colder, the low got drier, causing a shrinkage and retreat of the forests that had lavishly clothed the tropical zones in the very warm and moist times. The forest-living apes retreated with the forest and a new ecological niche began to open up, in the shape of spreading savannahs, for exploitation by a suitably evolved 'ex-ape'. From about 7 mya, the separation of the human line first from the gorillas and then from the chimpanzees was under way. It is at times of rapid environmental change that small populations of animals evolve fastest: the slightest advantage conferred by some random mutation may allow an individual to thrive better in a new niche and leave more descendants behind, themselves to thrive better than less well-adapted individuals. And so genetic lines are selected by nature and perpetuated.

Human Origins

It is not in caves that the evidence for the evolution of our earliest ancestors in the human line is to be found – as we have seen, scarcely a cave from times as far back as 6 mya survives. They would not have wanted to be confined in caves in any case, though no doubt their carcasses sometimes found their way into caves that formed part of other creatures' lairs. These remote ancestors of ours frequented the stands of trees that were maintained along watercourses where food, both vegetable and to some extent animal, might be found. Erosion out of the deposits of old river valleys in East Africa has turned up skull fragments and even limb bone pieces of 'ex-apes' who were shedding their more ape-like traits and evolving towards the bipedal walking-on-two-legs mode of the human line. Continuing forest shrinkage during these ongoingly dry and coldish times was extending the range of the grassland habitat and our remote ancestors were standing up on two legs in it - if only at first to be able to run back to the shelter of the remaining trees. Finds from Kenya and Ethiopia cover a time span from about 5.5 to 4 mya to shed light on these human beginnings.

Evidence turns up more widely in Africa after 4 mya, showing a trend to brain size now going beyond the ape range in absolute terms and big in any case for the body sizes indicated, up to about 1.25 m in height. These creatures are likely to have been capable of the sort of limited tool use seen in chimp hands today, though as with the chimps the materials employed were mostly of a perishable nature and very little modified. In South Africa the fragmentary fossils of these early ape-men are sometimes found in caves of around 3 mya, but almost certainly not because they lived in them (they probably still slept in what trees they could find and their hand and foot bones show they were still practised climbers); rather their remains were taken back to the caves by the more ferocious beasts that preyed on them. In one case it looks as though a leopard was in the habit of chewing up its prey, which included some of these proto-humans, in a tree that grew over a cave fissure: the complete skeletons of an apeman and a leopard are now coming to light during painstaking excavation, which rather suggests that the leopard ended up chasing an apeman over the edge and both perished in the cave below.

The passage of time brought bigger brains, more human-looking teeth and fuller bipedalism until, about 2.4 mya, the archaeological record shows a definite association of deliberately knapped stone tools alongside the bones of their makers – in fact, stone tools found away from any association with proto-human fossils go back a little further in time. In making stone tools to a regular pattern, however simple at first, these creatures were doing something that today's apes struggle and fail to do even under instruction. Meat eating is attested by the added association of deliberately broken animal bones, running at a rate above the occasional level seen among chimps. Some at least of the tools were being used to butcher meat. The sheer efficiency of meat eating as a mode of nutrition, especially to fuel big brains, was vital to human evolution. The sharing of meat that had been cooperatively acquired, whether by scavenging or hunting, was a cornerstone of human social development in a feedback process that promoted complex social relations and fed the big brains that could handle them.

The Beginnings of Humanity

Toolmaking suggests the use of some form of speaking. Both involve a process of logic through time, with the accomplishment of steps along the way to the goal of the finished tool or the finished expression. From an early stage, there is moreover evidence of 'handedness' (usually right-handedness) in the production of the tools and humans are the only markedly 'handed' primates, which goes with a certain assymmetry of our brains that is also associated with speech; meanwhile our upright posture, a concomitant of bipedal walking, has facilitated the evolution of the chest musculature and throat anatomy necessary to produce the sounds of speech. Speech and the development of language in all its rich complexity have played such a crucial part in the creation of humanity.

Meat eating, toolmaking and ground living were the trinity of adaptations that set our remote ancestors on the way to full humanity. Ground living, of course, brought its dangers which only quick-witted resourcefulness could avoid. On some sites, collections of unworked rocks suggest the stockpiling of throwing stones to see off the wild enemies of these proto-humans: the stones also indicate the likely place of these people in the natural order, as second-level scavengers following the big predators (like lions) around and scaring off the first line of scavengers (hyenas) with their throwing stones.

At the point we have now reached in the human story, about 2.5 mya in rather cold and dry times, there is no unambiguous evidence of the making of 'home bases' with any sort of built structures or of the use of fire: nothing like the repertoire of the cave people of some million years and more later. But the quality of the stone tools got very slowly better and we can speculate that language use was making similarly slow progress. By about 2 mya, if not before, some of these early humans were beginning to spread out of Africa into the wider world, via the region of the Red Sea and the Near East and along the southern shores of the Mediterranean.

The classification of proto-human types identified in the African fossil record before these times of expansion is very complicated and contentious and prone to shift with new discoveries, but by 1.8 mya at least we have arrived at a form of humanity, increasingly worldwide in its scope, that we can conveniently assign to a single genus and species: *Homo erectus*. There is a particular specimen of *H. erectus* from East Africa, a young man, whose nearly complete skeleton illustrates for us this stage of human evolution at about 1.6 mya, where everything below the skull was more or less of a form and stature like our own, while the brain in the heavily-built skull above remained about one-third smaller in volume than our average. The tall physique of such examples of the *erectus* species as this 'Nariokotome Boy' amply justify the species name: *H. erectus* was the great upright strider of the savannah.

Out of Africa

The spread of the *Homo erectus* stage of human evolution around the world looks pretty rapid, with the telescoping hindsight available to us, and it must be ranked as something of an achievement for these small-brained, Old Stone Age foragers to have reached the Far East by about 1.8 mya. At around 800,000 years

Before the Present (BP), they were able to inhabit an island in the Java Sea that can only ever have been reachable by a sea-crossing, a fact which bears witness to the range of technology in perishable materials that obviously accompanied the manufacture of stone tools: we are contemplating fibre-lashed rafts in this instance.

In the East, early stone tools never achieved the sophistication we see in some of the artefacts later made in Africa and Europe, although the very oldest tools from European sites are also of the simplest kind. It may be the case that it was a very early form of *H. erectus*, neither so big-brained nor long-limbed as the 'Nariokotome Boy', who carried the human line into Europe (and Asia, for that matter). Early humans seem to have reached the West European hinterland of the Mediterranean after 1 mya (although they were in Georgia in the east by 1.8 mya). At the Spanish site of Gran Dolina in the Sierra de Atapuerca and dated to about 780,000 BP, some teeth and skull fragments together with hand and foot bones belong to four individuals whose scattered remains have prompted thoughts of cannibalism in some anthropologists' minds. Simple stone tools were found there too, as they have been at slightly older sites (by up to 100,000 years BP) in Italy, France and Germany, in some cases with further fragments of human fossils. Tools as old as 700,000 BP have been found near Lowestoft in England. Better made stone tools in the evolving African fashion, often showing a symmetrical stylishness in the typical 'hand-axe' form that we can still admire (and most of us would not easily be able to imitate), arrived in Europe at around 600,000 BP – at a time when the climate was taking a decided turn for the worse with the onset of one of the major glaciations of the last half-a-million or so years. The fact of the continued presence of early humanity in parts of Europe during these harsh times is inconceivable without the occupation of rock shelters and caves and the control of fire.

The earliest evidence for the taming of fire comes from Africa at around 1.5 mya, in the form of baked earth with lumps of burnt clay in association with stone tools. The degree of baking indicates temperatures higher than could have been generated naturally by grassland fires. Sometimes these early scenes of fire control display positively hearth-like arrangements of stones together with placements of larger stones that suggest the anchoring down of wind-breaks. The idea of constructed shelter around the fire was evidently in the air in Africa at an early date.

In ice age Europe, rock overhangs and caves provided ready-made shelter and there are signs at sites in France and Germany that, here too, a certain amount of added construction was employed at an early date to improve on the natural shelter of these locations: at a cave site near Nice a hearth-like focus of early human activity with burnt mussel shells may be interpreted as surrounded by larger stones that perhaps held down some wooden-poled screen of animal skins.

By about 500,000 BP, the slow but steady evolution of humanity was producing, in Africa and Europe at least, bigger-brained versions of humanity that go by the name of *Homo heidelbergensis* after the German city near which an example – a massive jaw – was found many years ago. The site of this find was not a cave but a gravel pit, and the slightly younger (450,000 BP) remains of 'Boxgrove Man' (from a site near Chichester in Sussex) do not come from a cave either and date to a warm interlude of the ice age era. Of about the same age, but this time from a cave (albeit collapsed) in the Mendips in Somerset, are some rather crude stone tools in poor quality stone; better made tools from Kent's Cavern in Devon were probably washed into the cave from open-air sites. The splendid shin bone of 'Boxgrove Man' was found in the company of some finely knapped flint hand-axes that were used to butcher the giant deer, rhinos and horses of the time: a horse's shoulder blade looks as though it suffered piercing with a spear. Of about the same period from Clacton in Essex comes a pointed wooden spear tip that may attest to the hunting prowess of its makers, unless it is really a digging stick to get up plant food or even a snow probe for the cold winters of those years. What certainly appear to be spears come from a coal mine in Germany: they were evidently employed in the hunting of horses about 400,000 years ago. Real hunting of prey was taking its place beside scavenging, or overtaking it.

Cave-dwelling

One of the world's oldest surviving cave sites able to draw a picture of the life of the cave dwellers of half-a-million years ago is Zhoukoudian, near Beijing. In a period around 450,000 BP, when northern China was enjoying a climate about as warm as it does today (which means it could be very cold in winter), the inhabitants of Zhoukoudian warmed themselves with fires which have left thin lenses of ash in the cave deposits containing concentrations of charred bones and seeds. In the cold northerly world of ice age times, fire brought so many blessings to evolving humanity: warmth and the deterrence of foes; thawing, cooking and smoking of meat; light to prolong the labours of the day like toolmaking beyond the allowance of the hours and seasons of nature; focus for the all-important social relations of food-sharing, care of the young, mutual grooming and language development. The first glimmerings of the family and the clan were perhaps lit up around the firesides of those remote days.

At Zhoukoudian, the remains of some forty individual people have been discovered in the Lower Palaeolithic levels of this cave and the damaged state of their bones suggests cannibalism again. This disturbing trait of human behaviour is quite often attributed to the fossil remains of our remote forbears and it has an interest beyond the morbidly sensational. For the fact is that, except in unusually stressed circumstances, people can almost always find something better to eat than people. Where cannibalism has been regularly practised in recent times it has always been for non-utilitarian reasons: something to do with ideological beliefs about absorbing the qualities of others, say, or seeing off their spirits. So a hint of cannibalism in the distant days of early human evolution might just point to the emergence of ideas of some sort in the enlarging brains of our prehistoric forerunners. There is precious little else to indicate any imaginative side to these remote people, once we have acknowledged the skill – even 'artistry' – of some of their stone tool production.

CHAPTER 3

The Neanderthal Era

The possibly cannibalistic cave people of Zhoukoudian belonged to the *Homo erectus* species. Some of their contemporaries in Africa and Europe were already heading in the direction of later stages of humanity. In Africa, the ultimate evolution of *Homo sapiens sapiens* has been suggested by several fossil finds. In Europe, types like *H. heidelbergensis* may represent the last common ancestor between *H. sapiens sapiens* and *H. sapiens neanderthalensis.* Genetic studies on the remains of a growing range of Neanderthal individuals have been held to indicate that our own ancestors and those of the Neanderthalers parted company (ceased to breed together very much, if at all) at around 500,000 BP. There are sites in the French Pyrenees and in Greece that, towards 400,000 BP, reveal the first distinctive developments of the Neanderthal type, though as yet without the impressive brain capacity of the full Neanderthal specimens.

Meanwhile the development of a new toolmaking concept spread from its African origins to Europe around 250,000 BP: it is called the Levallois technique after the Paris suburb where it was first noted in the early days of palaeolithic archaeology. 'Concept' is the appropriate word, since the practice calls for considerable flint knapping forethought in preparing the raw material up to a point where one final blow suddenly reveals the finished tool as the last preparatory piece falls away. This foresight implies the ability to imagine in advance what the completed work will have produced, and it is tempting to think that language use and thought processes were advancing in step with this imaginative achievement. The Levallois technique was not employed everywhere and at all times, but its place in the repertoire does witness to mental progress. Interestingly, in the Far East stone technology remained relatively simple through these times: wood, perhaps bamboo, which could not survive in the archaeological record, may have been the raw material of choice for the enduring *H. erectus* populations of that part of the world. Stray finds of wooden implements in Europe point to general use of this obvious, but largely perishable, material. Bone and antler implements, which would often have survived if made in any quantities, do not seem to have been much in use anywhere in the world at this stage.

In Europe, the ongoing trend towards the Neanderthal type of humanity is evident at sites (neither of them caves) like Steinheim in Germany and Swanscombe in England; the skull from the latter shows a respectable 1325 ml of brain volume at about 250,000 BP. Of about the same age in Spain, the deposits of a cave system in the Sierra de Atapuerca have yielded up the remains of at least thirty people of both sexes, some of them children. One of them has a brain volume of 1390 ml (well within the modern range) and some very Neanderthal skull features, like pronounced bony brow arches over the eyes and that general Neanderthal look of the face's having been, as it were, pulled forward by the (large) nose and inflated in the cheeks. There are signs in the postcranial skeleton remains here that the squat and shortish body pattern of the Neanderthalers was emerging too. No stone tools were found in association with these human fossils, which suggests that these caves were being used as the lairs and dumping places of predatory carnivores that sometimes made human kills. It is just possible, however, that the people were using the caves as a disposal site for their own dead: even some tiny finger bones were found. A quarter-of-a-million years ago would be a very early date for such a very human practice.

The typical tool kit of the Neanderthalers, based largely on broad flakes of flint, can be seen to have been evolving at various sites on Jersey and in France and Belgium back beyond 200,000 BP, in a period probably belonging to a warmish interstadial of the last ice age but one. (Interstadials are the shorter and mildly warmer interludes within ice ages, while interglacials are the substantially warmer and longer periods between ice ages.)

The Neanderthal Type

The compact body shape of the classic Neanderthalers of the last ice age, with big chests and short extremities, was an evolutionary strategy to conserve heat, a bit reminiscent of the Eskimo physique in some ways and for similar reasons. They probably sported heavy heads of hair, too, though there is no reason to depict them as hairy 'ape men' all over: they were no more ape men than we are and almost certainly wore clothing of some sort in their harshly cold world. Naturally, no clothing from this period could have survived, but it must have been simple kit since needles to sew and toggles to secure have not been discovered on Neanderthal sites – hides bound in place with rawhide thongs or strings of vegetable matter seem most likely. (Human beings have, according to genetic studies, been relatively hairless since about 1.7 mya, in the early years of *H. erectus*– except on the head, where a good mop of hair offered protection first against the fierce savannah sun and later on against heat loss in the cold.)

The Neanderthalers may well have been fair-skinned like the present-day natives of northern Europe, to derive maximum benefit from the vitamin enhancing ultraviolet light in whatever sunlight came their way. Their world may often have resembled the tundra of the frozen north today, but their years enjoyed the same seasonal lengths of day as we experience now in the same latitudes. For all their barrel-chested stockiness, the Neanderthalers' bodies below the neck were not so very different from our own: it was their heads, above all their faces, that marked them out from us. Heavily brow-ridged, rugged for the sake of powerful musculature, big jawed and big of teeth, these were faces made for tearing, gripping and chewing – both of meat to eat and no doubt hides to soften up. Wear on the front teeth of some specimens suggests the cutting up of meat or hides, clamped in the jaw, with flint flakes.

Neanderthal folk were clearly great meat eaters, not so much out of choice perhaps as out of necessity in the shape of what was available, what was most nutritious and what they were equipped to exploit. No doubt they foraged for plant food where it was available (and there are a few sites with pollen remains that indicate much resort to vegetable food) but there is equally no doubt that they predominantly ate meat, with the littered bones of their consumption of animals to prove it. Meat eating supplies a lot of energy fast but meat eating to excess has its health hazards, too, which are reflected in the condition of some Neanderthal bones. In general, the Neanderthal life could scarcely be a healthy or a long one. From the bones of the few hundreds of Neanderthalers we have recovered, we can see that life expectancy for males extended into the thirties, for females the twenties, with high infant mortality and every chance of injury or at least high physical stress in the course of their tough, brief lives. The arm and hand bones of the Neanderthalers were clearly suited to grasping and lifting heavy burdens while their leg and foot bones show signs of a lifetime of constant scrabbling about (rather random scrabbling at that): indeed it has been said that their bones carry patterns of wear and stress comparable to those seen today among rodeo riders. Theirs was a hard and, unsurprisingly, disease prone life. Even a case of lung cancer has been identified in a Neanderthal skeleton from a French site.

Neanderthal Behaviour

The average Neanderthal brain was bigger than the average modern brain, though the shapes and sizes of various parts of the brain were different from those of the same parts in modern people: in particular, they lacked the modern bulk of frontal neocortex. What those Neanderthal brains were capable of can only be judged from the archaeology that records some aspects of their behaviour. Of course, archaeology can hardly reconstruct every possible nuance of any past lives (for all we know the Neanderthalers might have brought choral performance to unmatched heights), but it can go a surprisingly long way in interpreting the whole range of material evidence people leave behind, sometimes in unexpected directions given the unpromising first appearances of the dry data. The variety and range shown by the tools of the Neanderthalers, called Mousterian after one of their first cave sites to be excavated in France, suggests a more sophisticated mental achievement than we see in their predecessors. (Incidentally the tools being made contemporaneously by non-Neanderthal folk in Africa were broadly similar.) To go with the improved technology, we can speculate that language was more sophisticated, too. The vocal tracts of the Neanderthalers may look a little limited in the gamut of sounds they could produce, but only a little, and by this stage of human evolution it must have been the brain's capacity that determined the level of speech and language use available. The more sophisticated the modes of speech, the more sophisticated the social relations in play. The Neanderthal folk were living in small social groupings, evidently not going very far to get their food or find their raw materials. They foraged, they scavenged and they hunted – sometimes scavenging more than hunting, perhaps, though they certainly hunted in an organized way often enough, as exploits like driving horses over cliffs testify. Scavenging, normally a potentially dangerous way of acquiring meat because bacteria have had time to get to work, was something the Neanderthalers were well placed to carry on in the often cold and antiseptic world of their time – in a way that none of their wild animal competitors could do. The frozen carcasses of animals perhaps killed by other predators or by cold and hunger could be dragged home to the cave and thawed out by the fire: bones of horses, deer and reindeer, with other creatures, litter the living floors of Neanderthal occupation sites. The distribution of those relics of their meals, in a demonstration of what archaeology can potentially help us to discover, has suggested to some scholars that the hunting males may have hogged their catches in their own semi-segregated parts of the caves, while females and infants made do with less meaty food in their separate areas. What relations between the sexes were like is hard to know at this distance along with any clues as to the social hierarchy and 'tribal' interactions of these people. Neanderthal children matured physically more quickly than ours do, their brains growing fast in skulls that could at an early age take on the distinctive pulled-forward and rugged look. A four-year-old child from a cave at Gibraltar had a brain as large as many a modern adult at 1400 ml, while a nine-year-old boy from Uzbekistan already sported 1500 ml, at the top of the average modern range. The oddly adult children of the Neanderthal folk must have experienced a curtailed childhood as far as play and learning were concerned by comparison with our own: there was less to learn and the Neanderthal mind, on the assumption that anything like our own imaginative consciousness existed among them, was hardly filled with the sort of ideological baggage that our minds cannot escape – however good in their way at toolmaking, food procurement and the social niceties these people may have been. It has been said of the Neanderthal people, as evidenced by their products and even the rather haphazardly worn state of their bones, that they must have lived in the same sort of eternal present – without much memory or forethought or purpose – that the chimps inhabit, whose mental world seems to be reinvented every fifteen minutes; every day, perhaps, with the Neanderthalers.

Modern Types and Modern Ways

The Neanderthalers were in undisputed possession of the caves of Europe and Western Asia from the times of the Last Interglacial well into the duration of the Last Glaciation, until around 30,000 years ago (when there were about 20,000 more years of ice age to go). Undisputed by other sorts of people, that is – for there were fierce rivals to the Neanderthalers in the animal world to fight with them over the possession of the caves. But in Africa there are signs that their eventual successors were emerging during the long millennia of the Neanderthal occupation of Eurasia.

Firstly there appeared, perhaps as early as 200,000 BP and certainly by 160,000, people of a more modern physical appearance, with skulls that – even when they might still be rugged – lacked the distinctive panoply of Neanderthal features like the very heavy brow arches and pulled-forward, chinless faces. Genetic studies of modern human populations concur with the fossil evidence in dating the emergence of *Homo sapiens sapiens* to this time span, and possibly in Africa, with the evolution of an initially very small population. These more physically modern types show a broadness of skull over the ears that the Neanderthalers lack, with flatter faces and hollowed cheeks instead of forward inflatedness, and they sometimes display the beginnings of the modern human chin in contrast with the heavy roundedness of the front portion of the typical Neanderthal jaw. (When jaw size was reduced in our ancestors, the chin was needed to add strength at the front.)

For a long time the behaviour of these more modern-looking people in Africa, as evidenced in the archaeological record by what they left behind them, looks basically no different to us from what their Neanderthal contemporaries were doing in Eurasia. And then there emerge signs here and there of the innovations we associate with the Neanderthalers' Upper Palaeolithic successors in Europe. Instead of stone tool kits based on broad flakes of flint, there are episodes of toolmaking in the form of elongated blades. A cave site in South Africa shows narrow blade tools in layers above (and consequently a bit later than) levels in which the remains of some slender-limbed people were found who lacked heavy brow-ridges and sported real chins, albeit with very large teeth, at a period between 115-75,000 BP. So here we have a case, at Klasies River Mouth, of an early site with first more modern physical types and then more modern tools that foreshadow later developments. Blade tools have been excavated in Morocco with a date of 70,000 BP. With claimed dates of about 90,000 BP, there are odd finds of sophisticated bone tools, including barbed harpoons from Zaire, that also prefigure the complex cultures of ice age Europe in post-Neanderthal times. A site called Blombos Cave in South Africa, dated to 75,000 BP, has given us deliberately perforated seashells that were evidently made for non-utilitarian reasons, and pieces of ochre engraved with rather purposeful lines and hatchings that similarly anticipate the art of the Crô-Magnon people who came after the Neanderthalers in Europe. Considerably older are the same sort of perforated shell beads discovered in Israel (in caves at Mount Carmel) and in Algeria: both in a date range from 100 to 135,000 BP. The beads were presumably made as items invested with ideological significance and desirability. Maybe they were gifted or 'traded' to strengthen social and proto-economic relationships. Perhaps they were worn as markers of identity, to do with ethnicity or rank or at least as personal, possibly sexual, decoration. It has been observed that the appearance of personal decoration marks the arrival of the sense of 'self' in differentiation from all others: a momentous stage in the evolution of human consciousness.

In the case of the Levantine finds, these beads were being made by people the rest of whose material culture – tool kits based on flakes rather than blades – was indistinguishable from that of their Neanderthal contemporaries. They do appear, however, to have occasionally furnished burials of their dead with 'grave goods' in the shape of animal parts (a boar's jaw, a deer's skull and antlers) in a way that Neanderthalers probably did not. One of them, incidentally, may have died of a spear thrust to the hip. The Algerian beads belonged to an essentially similar flake tool culture, too. In all cases, the perpetrators of these outbreaks of modern behaviour, where their bones have been found, were also more modern physical types of a long-limbed warm-adapted character like our own ancestors. But their behaviour was not wholly or continuously modern. So such instances of innovation that look towards the Upper Palaeolithic can be seen in their early manifestations as rather sporadic essays in more modern behaviour – beads here, blade tools there, occasional grave goods, scraps of design doodling – that came and went against a patchy background of little or no major cultural change for many millennia. It may be that the use of language as the complex medium of abstract thought that we know was itself very slow to evolve too – but when it really took off it was to facilitate the integration of the whole range of human capabilities in a way that would change the world forever.

The Spread of the Moderns

While the Neanderthal folk were still going strong in Eurasia, with thirty thousand years or more before them, the moderns of Africa were beginning to spread their physical type out of the vast continent of their birth into the rest of the world. It was a spectacularly rapid and successful venture, in hindsight and in light of the enormity of what they achieved. Their preferred route out of Africa, accomplished after about 70,000 BP, seems to have been to cross the southern end of the Red Sea at the Bab-el-Mandeb Strait and carry on along the Indian Ocean coast of Saudi Arabia to the Persian Gulf and thence to India and on to the Malay Peninsula and Australasia. They were in southern Australia by 45,000 BP.

After that early occupation of the Levant at around 100,000 BP, with modern humans in place but not doing anything very modern that we can see in the archaeological record, the same caves went over to Neanderthal occupation without any traces of modern behaviour at all. The Neanderthalers arrived there at about 60,000 BP, probably to escape a fresh onset of cruelly cold times in Eastern Europe, along with brown bears, wolves and woolly rhinos. They were to last in the Levant until about 40,000 BP, without any innovations in their way of life. (It is worth noting, however, that some of these latter-day Neanderthal denizens of the Mount Carmel caves were among the tallest, biggest-brained and perhaps least classically Neanderthal types of their time. One male adult had a cranial capacity of 1740 ml, the largest of any fossil human, including all the early moderns. He lived somewhere between 50-40,000 years ago and his people may have seen a degree of interbreeding with incoming moderns in the Levant.)

The moderns reappeared in the Levant at about 50-45,000 BP and by then they were displaying a range of modern cultural traits with a developed blade technology. The development of this Upper Palaeolithic culture perhaps took place in south-west Asia – from where it was also poised to make its way into Eastern Europe, during a warmer lull in the very cold times of the last ice age. The moderns and their Upper Palaeolithic mode of life were to infiltrate territory in Europe hitherto in the sole possession of the

Neanderthal folk who had occupied it, thanks to their cold-adapted physiques and accommodation to its harsh ecology, for a hundred thousand years.

CHAPTER 4

The Ice Age World

The world in which the classic types of European cave people of the last ice age – the Neanderthal folk and their Crô-Magnon successors – lived and died and created their various cultures was a severe one indeed. Though it was not without its warmer interstadials, some of them of respectable duration, it was averagely colder than today and for long stretches much colder. The alterations that the glaciation of the northern latitudes and of the mountain ranges further south could bring included changes of temperature, of wind force and direction, of precipitation (snow or rain), of vegetation and animal life and of sea levels and coastlines.

Before the last ice age got under way, the time of the Last Interglacial had been markedly warmer than today, though we are headed back to very warm conditions again in pretty short order as global warming proceeds.

The glaciers of the north and of the mountain ranges like the Alps receded as they are doing now and sea levels, with globally melting ice, reached just a little higher than they stand today, so coastlines were broadly similar. By 120,000 BP things were warmer than they are now, which brought rhino, hippo and elephant together with lion and hyena even into northern Europe. That does not mean that the north was as warm and tropical as our equatorial lands are – simply that migration routes were opened up to permit the entry of these animals into Europe at a time when there were few human enemies to prey upon them and the hunting skills and technology of those people, the European Neanderthalers, were not up to doing so very much about them. Those Neanderthal folk were on the whole not quite as evolved into their classical form as they would be after the last ice age came down upon them, from about 110,000 BP. The first 30,000 years of the new glaciation saw a slow reversion to cold conditions in a sequence of shortish cold spells of varying intensity until about 80,000 BP when things got seriously and continuously cold again. Average temperature might by this stage be 10° C lower than today's, with stronger cold winds blowing and glaciers extending so that the conditions of the far north and of the mountain tops came south and down the mountainsides. Steppe and even tundra landscapes extended into what had been, and are today, scenes of oak mixed forest, relieved then only with patches of pine, birch and willow.

After 80,000 BP, it was too cold except in occasional warmer interstadials for people to live north of the Alps, but the small Neanderthal populations of more southerly Europe adapted to the cold new world with both some further physical evolution towards their rugged classic type and also with technological strategies to hunt a new fauna that pushed out the African contingent of interglacial times. By this time, the areas that would one day be Denmark, Holland and northern Germany were a treeless tundra or at best a taiga of sparse and stunted trees, even polar in today's terms in places. The glaciers of Scandinavia and the Alps came within 500 km of each other and loess storms (wind-blown dust from the steppe) made Central and Eastern Europe uninhabitable, except again in warmer interstadial episodes. South of the tundra in south-west Europe was a dryish steppe-like world with hardy trees like pine and birch here and there, while sheltered valleys might be quite wooded. Dry land was extended out beyond the present coastline by the lowering of sea level now that so much of the globe's precipitation was locked up in the ice of the glaciers. Land extended out into the Bay of Biscay, for example, and Britain was connected by a substantial land-bridge (some of it under the ice) to continental Europe. We talk of steppe and tundra but it must be remembered that these European environments of the ice age were not, though they resembled it, in the Arctic: the lengths of the days and the angles of the sunlight were the same as they are here now and summers could still be long and quite warm if drier than today.

Wildlife and Food Supply

All in all, circumstances favoured the flourishing of a rich range of wildlife, on which the Neanderthal people preyed. The tundra and taiga were especially rich in game including reindeer, musk ox, wolf, arctic fox, glutton, ermine, stoat, with rodent and bird life of many kinds. Mammoths and woolly rhinos added a bulky and meat-rich component to the mix. Many of these creatures migrated south in winter to the fringes of the woods that themselves harboured red deer, brown bear, lynx, marten, beaver, hyena, bison and aurochs (wild cattle) with mice, voles and lemmings in large numbers. In fact it was not so easy to hunt in the woods as it was in the tundra and taiga and nor were they so well stocked. Even the loess steppe of Central and Eastern Europe, uninhabitable in the coldest and driest times, could in the summers of the interstadials grow grass to support many rodents and also some bigger animals like horses and hyenas, sometimes reindeer, mammoths and predatory lions. Further east, a proper steppeland with all these denizens stretched away into Asia.

The lions were a serious threat to the struggling bands of human hunters and scavengers, especially in their cave-lion version, which was a quarter larger than the African lion of today and liked to make its lair in the same caves as the Neanderthal people favoured for their homes. Commoner, though, and just as threatening was the cave-bear, bigger at 2.7 m long than a grizzly bear of our times. Cave-bears hibernated in the caves and probably disputed them with their human rivals more often than the lions did, and with uncertain outcome: one Austrian cave contained the remains of 30,000 bears, of long and obviously secure tenancy. These bears may have been primarily herbivorous but, like their Neanderthal contemporaries, they probably ate meat too – in greater quantity than bears do today. The dens of cave-hyenas of the ice age show that they carried on their scavenging way of life in a big way.

As with the cave-frequenting lions, bears and hyenas, Neanderthal people found caves made a better home than open-air sites ever could. They were certainly better places as far as the archaeological preservation of Neanderthal (and later) products goes, and cave sites are easier for us to find, too. The limestone caves of the Périgord region of south-west France made particularly good homes: often sited up the sides of small river valleys that gave shelter from the weather (south facing, then as now, to be preferred for sunshine and wind avoidance), elevation above flooding and good prospects up and down the valley to keep an eye on the movement of potential prey, with flint supplies to hand. This area of France was near the Atlantic Ocean (though ice age sea level fall extended the land out into what is now the Bay of Biscay) and consequently enjoyed cooler summers than the lands further east into the continent. This cooler year-round temperature allowed extensions of the steppe and even tundra of more northerly parts to reach over the higher plateaux of the region, replete with the rich game that went with those conditions. The high year-round levels of sunshine favoured the growth of the ground plants needed by herds of reindeer, bison and horse. Meanwhile, winters were not so harsh that, in the valleys, patches of woodland could not keep a hold below the barer plateaux. The east to west slopes of the Massif Central down to the Atlantic Ocean made for a rapid gradient of ecologies so that the animal life of the times did not need to migrate very far with the seasons and people never had to go far for their food at any time of the year.

Living Quarters

The caves of the Neanderthal folk, chosen for their shelter, security and vantage, sometimes show signs of improvement with the construction of added walling. We have seen that some hints of built structure go back much earlier than Neanderthal times in Europe – along with the anchoring of tent poles, there are even suggestions of the use of seaweed as bedding and wolf pelts as blankets inside the 'tents'. Evidence has been interpreted in a cave in the Périgord to indicate that, again in pre-Neanderthal times, there was a demarcation between a working area in the light of the cave mouth, a cooking area further in and a sleeping area along the dark north wall at the back of the cave. Neanderthal occupation of a cave in Spain features a low dry stone wall across the narrow part of the cave mouth and a 2 m length of similar dry stone walling, only 25 cm high, is attributed to Neanderthal handiwork in a French cave of the Dordogne Valley, while a height of 70 cm is recorded in another instance. A semicircular wall piled up out of reindeer antlers is claimed for yet another French Neanderthal cave.

The frequently encountered layers of ash and hearth places of the Neanderthalers' sites remind us that in their day fire had long since been tamed and its artificial ignition was understood. A cave at Krapina in Croatia has given us an example of what is claimed to be a fire-making twirl-stick in the form of a charred piece of birch wood from a Neanderthal context. But it has to be said that until the latter days of the Neanderthal folk, their fires were rather disorganized affairs, not contained in clearly structured hearths and not of very long duration to judge by the extent of ground penetration their heat effects achieved. We have already noted the suggestion that the Neanderthalers used their fires to thaw out scavenged meat in a uniquely human adaptation to ice age circumstances, and there is some indication that they stored joints of meat in pits on occasion.

The built improvements that the Neanderthal people sometimes incorporated in their caves testify to their constructional capabilities, which they also brought to bear on the creation of camp-sites away from their caves. Such open-air sites have been found up on the plateaux of south-west Europe, where they probably served as temporary bases for scavenging or acquiring raw materials when they were not simply kill sites that required a lengthy exploitation. Further away across the North European Plain and into Central and Eastern Europe, where caves were fewer, these open-air camps were often, of course, the only homes the people had. The ones we have found were mostly located near water, both because people and animals congregated near this necessity of life and also because preservation is more likely at such spots away from the utterly wind-blown wide open spaces.

In the Ukraine, what was certainly a wind-break and may have been a large tent of the Neanderthalers has been excavated: an oval up to 8 × 5 m, mainly based on mammoth bones, enclosing a dense concentration of stone tools and animal bones with quantities of ash. There is rather more ash in the northern part of the oval, where people perhaps slept close to the fire. (Large animal bones were evidently a chief fuel for the fire, as happened among Britain's sparse Neanderthal population, too.) Similar circles of mammoth bones are known from Neanderthal sites in Poland, Rumania and the Caucasus, and there are post holes on a site in Germany and in a French cave.

Neanderthal Technology

The common 'denticulate' flint flake tools of the Neanderthalers look well suited to the woodworking implied by post holes, and woodworking there must have been, though next to nothing made in that perishable material could survive from the remote past. Microscope studies have revealed the use of some stone tools on wood and/or the hafting of flint tools in wooden handles. A yew wood spear from a Neanderthal site in Germany, which looks as if it had a fire-hardened tip, was found in the ribs of an elephant, a testament to both Neanderthal woodworking and hunting prowess at around 130,000 BP, during the Last Interglacial.

Of the Neanderthalers' stone tools that were not used for working wood, some were clearly projectile points, some were used in butchery and some for the scraping of hides. Some Neanderthal toolmaking traditions included 'hand-axes' that were smaller and neater versions of much older tool types, and also blunt-backed knives and chisel-tipped burins that were to be much commoner after Neanderthal times. The latest of the Neanderthal tool kits in Europe, exhibited a blade-making tendency along with a few other traits in common with the tools of the moderns, as we shall see. A broadly similar progress is seen in the tools of the Neanderthal people of the Levant, where the Mount Carmel caves constitute the other great success story of Neanderthal cave living. There, too, a more blade-based toolmaking tradition comes in towards the end of the Neanderthal presence in the region. But then we must remember that the more modern types who came and went in the Mount Carmel caves, before and after the Neanderthalers there, also deployed a tool kit basically no different from that of the Neanderthal folk until about 40,000 BP. The same was generally true of these times in Africa as a whole, except for those sporadic outbreaks of blade-making. The toolmaking traditions of the Neanderthal people do show some local and chronological variations, but as a whole the Neanderthal tool kit was never anything like as rich or various or changeful as the Upper Palaeolithic cultures that came after it.

Neanderthal people simply were not doing as much with their tools as later people, or using them for such a variety of tasks. It is interesting to note that the animal bones found on their sites do not include those creatures whose capture needs snares, traps, hooks or prongs and we can conclude that they made none of these things, indeed had never thought of them. In general, the Mousterian tool kit found little place for bone and antler products. The amount of animal bones on Neanderthal sites is not large by comparison with later times and populations were evidently small, though it is possible that the hunters were in the habit of consuming the best part of their bag at their kill sites, without taking very much of it home to the caves – where women and children eked out their dole of meat with vegetable materials that could include aquatic plants, pine cones, vetch, wild peas, sea-beet, with some molluscs and fish. At some of the open-air kill sites there is a heavy concentration of the bones of just one species of prey, with the tools used in butchery lying among the bones.

Death and Burial

Hints of cannibalism dog the Neanderthalers as they do some of their predecessors. One of the first Neanderthal specimens to be found in the nineteenth century suggested it and finds at Krapina in Croatia in 1889 boosted the notion greatly: a mass of disarticulated and scattered bones, many of them of juveniles, some with long bones split open perhaps to get at the marrow, and some burned. Since, as we have already remarked, eating people is rarely an obvious nutritional resort, evidence like this points to a 'cultic' practice of some sort, which implies the existence of imaginative ideas in Neanderthal heads.

Cult and ideology is more certainly indicated by the burial practices of the Neanderthal cave people. The same Périgordian cave that gave the tools of the Neanderthal people the name of 'Mousterian' was also the site of one of the first Neanderthal burials to be excavated. At le Moustier the skeleton of a youth was found who had been buried in a 'sleeping position' on his right side with his right arm supporting his head, cheek to elbow, and apparently lying on a bed of flints. A fine hand-axe and some bones of reindeer and ox were discovered immediately before the human skeleton came to light, strongly suggesting that these items were grave goods deliberately buried with the youth to help him on his way in some Neanderthal afterlife. But not proving it – the axe and animal bones might only show that this Neanderthaler was simply buried in accidental proximity to a general scatter of occupation debris in the cave. Grave goods or no, he was certainly buried and burial in a home cave already suggests a certain ideological concern: if utilitarian disposal was all that was required, it would have been better done outside the home; apparently his fellows wanted to keep him near them, at least.

Various other sites have been proposed as scenes of Neanderthal burial cult. There are not so many of them and some belong to a late phase of the Neanderthal story. It should be remembered, moreover, that most of our Neanderthal specimens represent stray finds of fragmentary and isolated bones rather than deliberate burials. But real Neanderthal burials there are: the original find in the Feldhof caves of the Neander Dale in Germany concerned a Neanderthal burial (who had, incidentally, a deformed elbow joint, probably the result of a badly healed break). At la Chapelle in the Périgord a Neanderthaler was buried in what was clearly a rectangular cut pit and there are further such burials in the Crimea, the Levant, Iraq and Uzbekistan.

At Monte Circeo in Italy a Neanderthal skull, with the hole at its base enlarged – to get at the brains? – was once thought to have been placed at the centre of a small circle of bones like a shrine, but it may well have been an accidental and over interpreted arrangement. At Teshik Tash in mountainously remote Uzbekistan, the most easterly outpost of the Neanderthalers we know, a child's skeleton was claimed to be encircled with wild goat horns, and perhaps similar caution is called for. At Shanidar in Iraqi Kurdistan, a huge cave overlooking a river was the scene of many apparent burials, deliberate or accidental, with vivid stories to tell. There were the flexed skeleton of a very small child and the remains of eight adults. Five of these Neanderthalers were evidently deliberately buried and four were killed under rock falls. One of these latter individuals had had a colourful career: a blow at some time to the left side of the head had resulted in skull fracture and blinding in the left eye; his right arm had on some occasion been so badly injured that it wasted away and either came off or was removed; the right foot and leg had also sustained permanent injury. But, incredibly, all these wounds had healed and he had reached the ripe old age for a Neanderthaler of maybe about 40 when the rock fall laid him low. His deplorable condition suggests that, as in a few other instances, he must have had some help from his fellows to get as far as he did: these cases of sickly or crippled individuals tolerated and even, presumably, succoured by their fellows strongly point to the ongoing evolution of the human mental endowment. One of the undoubtedly deliberate burials at Shanidar was long considered to demonstrate the furnishing of grave goods at a Neanderthal burial: the bones were accompanied by a very high intensity of flower pollen, which may summon up scenes of grieving with floral tributes but has more prosaically been put down to high winds wafting in during the interment or subsequent burrowing by rodents covered in pollen.

Neanderthal Beliefs?

The clearest cases of deliberate burial with an ideological component come late in the Neanderthal story. The French site of la Ferrassie shows a whole 'family' of seven graves which might date back to 70,000 BP but may perhaps have been dug into older deposits by latter-day Neanderthal folk. La Ferassie is not a deep cave but rather a rock shelter with only a shallow overhang of rock. It lacks much evidence of general, everyday activity by Neanderthal people. Five of the graves are aligned east-west in a manner seen elsewhere: in this case the arrangement is in line with the overhang of the shelter. Of course, a south-facing cave sees the east to west traverse of the sun very well, with its connotations – for us – of birth and death. At the western end of the line of graves, two adults were buried head to head. The male of the pair (the one incidentally with leg bone anomalies that indicate lung cancer) was put into a shallow rectangular pit in flexed posture; the female skeleton was more tightly flexed and must have been bound in position. In the world of recent savage peoples, such tight flexing might point to an idea of the restraining of the dead to curtail their interference in the affairs of the living, but of course it also means you can dig a smaller grave. To the east of these adult graves there were two children's graves, also cut east to west. Further east there were nine pits with low mounds, one heaped over the remains of a very small infant – the others perhaps once harboured infant burials since lost. At the eastern end of the rock shelter were more pits and the remains of an infant whose body and skull were separated by about one metre, the latter under a triangular slab of rock with a shallow concavity on its underside surrounded by cup-like hollows in groups of two and four. This all looks like ideological belief of some sort, though we cannot tell what. A spread of limestone pieces over an area about 5 × 3 m has been seen as the floor of some possibly tent-like temporary structure. It is easy, but perhaps unwarranted, to imagine scenes of funereal grieving in the family vault, as it were, of some very unlucky (even by Neanderthal standards) little line of loved ones.

Those cup-like hollows apart, there is precious little trace of anything we could call art in all the output of the Neanderthalers, and certainly no representational art. Pieces of manganese dioxide and iron oxide with colouring potential have been found in Neanderthal contexts, but they were not used for drawing any design that we know or colouring up the bodies of the dead, as was sometimes done by Upper Palaeolithic people. Maybe the Neanderthalers coloured the skins they wore on their own living bodies. But there is one Neanderthal trait that really does substantiate the possibility of a consciously imaginative side to their character. They appear to have entertained some sort of cult of the cave-bear.

Bears and Men

It has been pointed out that the physique of the Neanderthalers, stocky and barrel-chested, was in itself rather bear-like. Bears meanwhile, especially when rearing up on their hind legs, possibly outdo even the great apes in their human resemblance, as the perennial popularity of teddy bears attests. Evidently that resemblance did not escape the Neanderthal mind – and, after all, the two species, man and beast, were fated to haunt the same caves during the cold of the ice age. The cave-bears, unmatched in the ferocity of the threat they posed to humans, were no teddy bears, however. Their need to hibernate in the caves in winter, just when the Neanderthalers also needed them most, must have led to countless confrontations – though the bears might be killed while hibernating. At all events, bears must have loomed large in the Neanderthal mentality wherever there were a lot of them about. Some Alpine caves, unsurprisingly not frequented by Neanderthalers, contain tens of thousands of bear bones. At the Drachenloch cave system in the Swiss Alps, Neanderthal tools were found near the entrance and, further in, there was evidence of a fire near which a 1 m square box-like arrangement of stones had evidently been constructed, with a 'lid' in the form of a single slab. In the 'box' there were seven bear skulls with their muzzles – according to the report of their discovery in the 1920s – pointing back towards the cave entrance.

The presence of bits of vertebrae with two of the skulls suggested that the bears had been decapitated and their heads put in the 'box' while still warm, as it were. At the back of a further cave of the system there was a shelf-like line of stone blocks on which six more bear skulls were artfully arranged on top of a couple of shin bones – one of the skulls had a thigh bone through the arch of its cheek, the whole thing resembling nothing so much as a 'skull and crossbones' for bears. But no tools of the Neanderthalers were found in association with all these bear remains, and give or take the blocks and 'box', the scene might simply have been created by the rummaging of bears among their own bones. The same could be said for some other sites proposed for a Neanderthal 'bear cult' but there is one place that cannot be written off and makes us think twice about writing off the rest. At Regourdou in the Périgord, to accompany a Neanderthal grave under a cairn of stones which included some bear bones, there is a mass bears' grave in the form of a stone-lined rectangular pit with the remains of more than twenty brown bears (one skeleton complete except for its skull) under a stone slab weighing a tonne. Collections of bears' teeth have been reported at other sites, as are very occasional collections of quartz crystals and sea shells.

Upper Palaeolithic Beginnings

Plainly the Neanderthal folk were endowed with minds that could, up to a point, bring the outside world – parts of it, at least – into their own imaginations. They produced no art that has survived them, but neither did the early moderns of Africa and the Levant. All these people, down to about 50,000 BP, were mostly making the same old tools and all there is to distinguish the early moderns from the Neanderthalers is represented by those sporadic outbreaks of blade-making, shell piercing, maybe of harpoon carving, the occasional furnishing of grave goods and some hints that they may have hunted a bit more purposefully. All these people appear to have been living in their eternal present without much organized memory of the past or anticipation of the future. Their use of language no doubt proceeded along the same lines: perhaps in the end it was the expansion and elaboration of language that transformed human minds into the integrated engines of imagination which produced the astonishing cultural innovations of the Upper Palaeolithic, including the wonderful works of art we associate with the caves of France and Spain (to which they are not confined). Perhaps only some genetic mutation in the brain made all that possible, after 60,000 BP.

Be that as it may, a few sites in France that definitely date to the end of the Neanderthal line feature distinctly Upper Palaeolithic traits. Some late Neanderthalers, fully classic physical specimens with no hint of interbreeding with more modern types or genetic evolution of their own, deployed a blade-based flint technology and made decorative items by piercing and grooving shells and animal teeth. They made better-structured hearths for their fires, too, than hitherto. Until the association of Neanderthal bones with these particular archaeological remains was established, it was often thought that such sites belonged to a first wave of incoming moderns. The question now is whether late Neanderthalers like these had invented such progressive developments all by themselves and were thus among the pioneers of the Upper Palaeolithic, or had somehow copied them from the first Upper Palaeolithic people on their scene. If it was only the latter case, then at least we know that the Neanderthal folk were well enough mentally endowed to recognize better technology when they saw it and see some point in personal decoration.

We have seen that modern *Homo sapiens sapiens* had spread more than halfway round the globe by at least 45,000 BP. At about the same date, the moderns made their appearance in Europe, perhaps from south-western Asia and during a lull in the ferocity of the last ice age. A newly discovered site south of Moscow would seem to be one of the earliest of the Upper Palaeolithic manifestations in Europe, well before 40,000 BP.

CHAPTER 5

Upper Palaeolithic Life in Caves

After 60,000 BP there followed a series of climate fluctuations that brought the Neanderthalers' homeland towards milder times, but conditions became pretty cold again towards 45,000 BP. Thereafter came fifteen thousand years of warming, with oak mixed forest replacing the more open situation of colder and drier times. It was during the earlier part of this climatic amelioration that the moderns put in their appearance in northern Eurasia. Probably evolved in Africa after about 200,000 BP, the moderns were tall and slender people with bodies suited to warm conditions: in the early stages of their cultural development, they were hardly fit for the cold world of the north. So the warm interstadial between about 45 and 30,000 BP smoothed their way into Eastern Europe from south-west Asia, probably somewhere in the region of the Caspian Sea. By 30,000 BP, it was turning cold again with the very worst of the ice age still to come at around 18,000 BP.

By that late date the Neanderthalers would be gone and it might be doubted that they could ever have lived through it: the very last of them appear to have petered out in southern Spain at about 25,000 BP. By about 18,000 BP, on the other hand, the moderns had developed their Upper Palaeolithic culture to the point where they could survive and even thrive in the fullest harshness of the glaciation. Indeed, they extended the range of humanity into parts never reached before across Russia and Siberia – on the way to the Americas.

The moderns introduce themselves in the archaeological record with very little in the way of indications of modern behaviour. But by 45,000 BP, they had somehow undergone a cultural transformation that saw them pioneering varied and sophisticated blade-making techniques (in fact, a whole range of flint knapping innovations and ventures into bone and antler tool production) – and embarking on a tradition of artistic production that would be one of the glories of their long-lasting career on earth. It may be that, even with their inherently clever minds, it still took a long time to invent the Upper Palaeolithic outlook, the like of which had never been seen in the world before. It may be that the routine use of complex language required a long developmental period: and without complex language, it would have been impossible to achieve complex thought and the integration of all aspects of life into a unified consciousness for each individual with a shared code for handling ideas inside each mind and communicating them with the minds of others. What the unified consciousness made possible was thinking about one thing in terms of another, one whole lot of things in terms of one or more whole lots of other things: and seeing relationships between them that prompted innovatory courses of action. This analogizing capability gave *Homo sapiens sapiens* a competitive edge over all other sorts of humanity that might be still around, doomed for lack of it.

The Birth of Art

It looks as though the Neanderthal mind was slow to see relationships, analogies if you like, between the different topics that were handled in the separate compartments of their consciousness: toolmaking was toolmaking, hunting was hunting, sex was sex, eating was eating and so on: perhaps, without a subtle language endowment, there was no feeling of a single consciousness for a Neanderthal 'person'. The art that appears to arrive rather suddenly on the scene with the spread of the moderns and their Upper Palaeolithic way of life is inevitably the most striking of all their innovations. After those countless millennia of uninspired doodles at best (and precious few of them) we are suddenly faced with representational art in the archaeological record of *Homo sapiens sapiens*. We find it in the caves of Western Europe well before 30,000 BP and, at the other end of the human diaspora, we find it in Australian rock shelters from about 40,000 BP. Suddenly, as it seems, art was something that all the moderns could do. Perhaps a period of eloquent gesturing, drawing in the air, preceded the permanent carving, engraving and painting of images, and perhaps other areas of artistic endeavour were developing hand in hand with the graphic arts: it has been suggested – on the basis of wear – that the stalactites and stalagmites of the caves were sometimes pressed into service like giant xylophones, in mineral deposit rather than wood, to play tunes. Certainly there are bone flutes among the archaeological remains of the Upper Palaeolithic folk from an early date and pictures that show their use and the possible playing of stringed instruments. A dented mammoth skull may even have been played as a drum. As for representational art, a recently discovered piece of carving from that early Upper Palaeolithic site in Russia may, at 45,000 BP, be the oldest representation of a human head that we know. From a cave in Germany and dating to well before 30,000 BP comes an extraordinary carving of a creature blessed with a human body and a lion's head. This is doubly astonishing: the realistic carving of both the human and the animal features is impressive by itself; to have put them together in an imaginative synthesis is mind-boggling. What extravagant meaning could this imagery have had for its makers? Whatever it meant, it certainly meant something new in the world: a highly imaginative idea. There is full-scale cave painting at a similarly early date, best seen in the Chauvet cave in France, with many very naturalistic depictions of horses, rhinos, lions and at least one other case of a composite human-animal figure (in this case half bison).

From the first, these Upper Palaeolithic people were carving and drawing on stones, bones and ivory (after about 25,000 BP sometimes modelling in clay and baking the products) to create portable works of art and also engraving and painting on cave walls or occasionally modelling-up larger animal figures to create permanent works in caves. Sometimes these artistic productions were close to the open air and everyday life in shallow cave mouths, but at other times they were deep inside cave systems where people did not live, where indeed the profound mystery of the bowels of the earth must have affected them as it affects us to this day.

This Upper Palaeolithic cave art lasted a very long time indeed, twenty thousand years at least, and though it may all look of a piece to us, it inevitably went through its cycles of traditions and local variations, with certain hot spots of achievement in places like south-west France and northern Spain. Some of its finest productions belong to late phases of the last ice age, after the onset of the climatic worsening of about 18,000 BP. In all this long career, the art must have been undertaken with different motivations at different times and meant different things in different times and places.

The Meanings of the Cave Art

There are not, in fact, all that many depictions of human beings in the cave art and where they occur they are oddly distorted, almost caricatured, in a way that surprises us when we see how naturalistically the animals of those times could be rendered. Among the portable productions showing human beings, female figurines predominate with heavily emphasized secondary sexual characteristics – often huge breasts to the neglect of facial features, hands or feet. Among the considerable number of inevitably mysterious 'abstract' signs and markings (lines and boxes for example) are a proportion of schematic sketches of the human female pubic area. But overwhelmingly, the cave art of the ice age is devoted to the depiction of the animal world and mostly but by no means exclusively of the bulkier animals of the hunt. It is no wonder that hunting magic was among the first explanations advanced to meet the problem of accounting for the Upper Palaeolithic art, together with fertility magic. Shamanistic visionary trances, with or without mind-altering substances, and an elaborate code of symbolic gender dichotomizing of the world are among other 'explanations'. Theorizing will go on and possibly make progress: for the moment it is sufficient to observe that, whatever the motivations of the art, we are certainly faced with an explosion of imaginative creativity among the Upper Palaeolithic people that was wholly new in the world of human evolution. It is interesting to note, incidentally, that although there is no sign of writing during these times, there are markings on bone scraps that look very much like numerical notation: the recording of hunting tallies, perhaps; even phases of the moon have been suggested. Hand silhouettes among the wall paintings imply the idea of counting.

Though they met it with far greater mental resources than their predecessors, the world of the Upper Palaeolithic people was just as severe for long stretches as it had been for the Neanderthal folk. Indeed, it was severer after 18,000 BP, in a way that the Neanderthalers could probably only have dealt with by retreating south again. But the moderns were even able to increase their range, thanks to their large and well-heated hut structures whose remains have been found in Northern and Eastern Europe and away into Siberia. These huts were constructed out of scores of mammoth bones and on some sites there is evidence that after an initial period where all the huts of a community were the same size there then followed an aggrandizement of some huts over the rest: are we seeing here the origins of stratified society with 'chiefs' and perhaps 'medicine men' coming to the fore? At Kostienki on the Don the social enrichment that prompted such developments probably rested on an abundant salmon fishery: the Neanderthalers had not usually made much of fishing, though they did exploit marine resources on Gibraltar (which was, incidentally, one of their last refuges).

Bone needles make their appearance in the archaeological record at about 22,000 BP in Eastern Europe and 20,000 BP in the west, along with perforated toggles, which the Neanderthalers cannot be demonstrated to have made.

The fitted clothes of the moderns were evidently much better tailored than the wraps of the Neanderthalers. Remains found with human burials show that clothing could be decorated with fringes of beads and there is evidence that different dress codes were adopted by the sexes – another indication of the growing complexity of human society, and the growing sense of the conscious self.

There are more Upper Palaeolithic sites than ones of earlier periods. There were more people, more communities with more cultural diversification in space and time; raw materials were fetched or traded from further afield, which points to a wider social context than before. This situation of larger groups with more people in them, communicating with other groups over bigger areas, means that social life would have been more complex than before, putting a premium on brain capacity to deal with life at a new pitch of human interaction; it also means that language must have been better able to negotiate all the tricky confrontations of this very social existence.

Full Humanity

For a most vivid and enigmatic illustration of the new-found complexities of Upper Palaeolithic life we can look to an extraordinary triple burial of two men and a crippled girl, at the site of Dolni Vestonice in Moravia, which dates to about 27,000 BP. One of the men was buried arms linked with the young woman who was spinally deformed; the other, who had been pierced at the hip with a wooden spear and may have been wearing a wooden mask, was laid out with his hands at the pubic area of the girl, where red ochre had been splashed around. Many a scenario can be imagined to account for this scene: what is certain is that nothing like it is remotely conceivable before the inauguration of the modern mind!

Among all known foraging peoples, whether still extant in the world today or recorded in the history of world exploration, there are patterns of sexual, familial and social relations that the Upper Palaeolithic people – to judge by their archaeological remains – were apt to share: home life with the provisioning of wives and children by hunting males, food (especially meat) sharing with family and relatives, more or less monogamous and sustained sexual relationships with marriages outside the immediate group, extensive kinship systems and regularized alliances in a wider social context (which does not exclude warfare on occasion). For most of their career, at least, it is not clear that the Neanderthal (and earlier) folk displayed all these fully human traits so completely, if at all. So the question arises as to what, in Eurasia, the relations between Neanderthalers and Crô-Magnon people might have been and whether they fought or tolerated or even mated with each other. We have already seen that DNA evidence has been interpreted to suggest that the ancestry of all modern people all over the world substantially parted company from that of the Neanderthalers half-a-million years ago. But here and there archaeology has suggested the possibility of interplay between the two groups. That they lived in some of the same places at more or less the same time is clear.

In the Levant there is a sequence of comings and goings of the two forms of humanity, both with the same tool kits, and the last of the Neanderthalers there do show some possibly modern physical features like chin development, albeit in a general context of clearly Neanderthal character. But in Europe we find a definite association of clear Neanderthal types with an early version of the Upper Palaeolithic, with roots in the past but additionally featuring a good deal of blade-making, some use of bone and antler and personal decoration in the form of perforated animal teeth. One French site of this 'Chatelperronian' tradition has revealed a rough circle of eleven post holes enclosing a 4 m wide area part-paved with limestone slabs and including two well-constructed hearths. The holes were probably for a mammoth-bone structure along the lines of the huts of the moderns in Eastern Europe. Sites like this belong to the period of likely overlap between Neanderthalers and moderns in Western Europe: three such sites show an interleaving of the toolmaking traditions associated with the Neanderthal and Crô-Magnon folk, at around 34,000 BP, or a little earlier if we follow the latest refinements of radiocarbon dating. But there are no skeletal remains in this part of the world to even hint at interbreeding between Neanderthals and Crô-Magnonards.

In the Lebanon at around 44,000 BP and Bulgaria at 43,000 BP, to take a couple of the oldest instances of the Upper Palaeolithic blade-making tradition, the blades were struck from cores of flint prepared in a distinctive new way without local precedents which was to be taken on by all the Upper Palaeolithic blade-makers thereafter (in Croatia and Moravia before 35,000 BP, in south-west France and Spain by 34,000 BP). The Chatelperronian was different, with blade cores that look more like an adaptation of the Neanderthalers' old Mousterian style. The most obvious explanation for the Neanderthal adoption of their own blade culture, along with a few other Upper Palaeolithic trimmings including beads, is that they somehow absorbed the idea from true Upper Palaeolithic people as they filtered into their world. This interpretation has been contested, however, by archaeologists who think the evidence of interleaving of occupation layers is unsound: they argue that the Neanderthalers made their Upper Palaeolithic innovations all by themselves before physically modern

people (often called after the Crô-Magnon site in
France) appeared.

The End of the Neanderthal Folk

In Central and Eastern Europe the cultural transition
to the Upper Palaeolithic is also sometimes thought to
show occasional signs of admixture rather in the spirit of
the Chatelperronian. Some anthropologists believe that
certain Neanderthal physical traits are also sometimes
seen in the early modern types of these regions, to
do with dental characteristics and heavy brow-ridges,
for example. This raises the question of interbreeding
between moderns and Neanderthalers once again,
despite the genetic evidence against it. A case in Portugal
as late as about 25,000 BP has been held to hint at a
limited amount of interbreeding, in line with evidence
that pockets of Neanderthalers lingered on in the
Mediterranean region of southern Europe for a few
millennia after 30,000 BP. Even if these pointers to
a certain amount of reproductive activity between
the two peoples turn out to be justified, it may have

gone on to only a very limited degree. That would not necessarily mean it was insignificant in its effect: it is even possible that an injection of Neanderthal genetics into the modern line helped to kick-start the mental motor of the Upper Palaeolithic revolution.

The Neanderthal presence as such vanishes from the archaeological record after 25,000 BP – indeed it vanishes well before that in any meaningful form, as represented by significant quantities of their bones or tools. We need not envisage a war of extermination on the part of the moderns to rid themselves of their rivals: the simple truth is probably that the classic Neanderthalers just were not serious rivals at all. Perhaps all it took to see them off was a bit better hunting prowess on the part of the moderns, with a bit higher birth-rate and a bit lower level of infant mortality. (Their bones show them to have lived averagely longer and with less physical trauma.) All these advantages consorted with the more complex social relations that the moderns were able to sustain as they foraged further, fetched their raw materials from further afield, exploited the seasonality of their supplies better and ate a bigger range of foods. The animal remains on their sites, and some of the pictures they drew, attest to the greater variety of their provisioning. They simply out-competed the old Neanderthalers, and perhaps without much in the way of contact. In their last southern European refuge, it may have been just the drought that went with the coldest phase of the last ice age that ended the Neanderthalers' line

The deterioration of the climate after 30,000 BP may well have highlighted the differences between the Neanderthalers' and the early moderns' capabilities: for all that the Neanderthalers represented a reasonably successful physical and cultural adaptation to the cold of the last ice age and the taller and slenderer Crô-Magnon people's main ancestors came from warmer climes, the sheer cleverness of the latter gave them the edge. Indeed the moderns repeated this pattern all over the world, perhaps with a certain amount of interbreeding again, soon replacing any lingering pockets of *erectus*-derived populations across the globe. (One such especially interesting pocket has been identified on the Indonesian island of Flores, where an early form of *erectus* underwent dwarfing – as many isolated species of animals do – and endured until about 12,000 BP, apparently making surprisingly sophisticated tools.)

Cave Life in Britain

The earliest appearance of the Crô-Magnon type in Britain is marked by a jaw bone fragment from Kent's Cavern in Devon, found in association with blade tools and dated to about 31,000 BP. A few thousands of years younger is a skeleton accompanied by ivory ornaments, perforated shells, Upper Palaeolithic tools and a quantity of red ochre, that was found in the Paviland Cave in South Wales and long ago erroneously dubbed the 'Red Lady of Paviland'. The bones have long been known to belong to a young man who lived about 26,500 years ago: the ochre was perhaps used to restore the red warmth of life to the dead body. The paucity of Upper Palaeolithic remains belonging to this early phase of the moderns in Britain shows that occupation was sparse and intermittent at this time

– but then Neanderthal physical remains are restricted to one site, Ponteprydd Cave in North Wales, though the Mousterian tool types of the Neanderthalers are quite widely known in south-east England.

The glacial maximum of around 18,000 BP saw the northern ice sheet reach down over most of Ireland and across the Irish Sea, its southerly limit then running in an irregular line across from South Wales to Yorkshire and down what is now roughly the coastline of Lincolnshire and Norfolk, and from there across the North Sea to present-day north Germany, Denmark and beyond. Sea level was so low, as a result of much of the globe's precipitation being locked up in ice and snow, that a land-bridge south of the glaciation joined Britain firmly to the Continent, as it had done so often during the epoch of the ice ages. It was across this terrain that human beings retreated during the worst of the glaciations and made their way back to Britain when things warmed up again.

They seem to have returned to Britain at around 13,000 BP. Gough's Cave at the Cheddar Gorge in Somerset has produced an example of humanly worked red deer bone that dates to 12,800 BP, when a milder interstadial within the last ice age probably saw summer temperatures a little higher than today's but winters colder. A distinctive British version of the Upper Palaeolithic developed quite widely between 12,500-12,000 BP, with blade tools in stone and various productions out of red deer antler, animal bones and teeth and mammoth ivory (though the mammoth was on the way out, if not gone by this time). Awls, needles, harpoons, rods and holed 'batons' of uncertain use were made. This British Upper Palaeolithic is called 'Cresswellian' after the Cresswell Crags in Derbyshire where it has been found – in general Cresswellian finds are made in limestone country up from Devon, through Somerset and South Wales to Derbyshire, with a few stray finds in East Anglia and Kent. But there must have been numerous open-air camps as well as the caves where Cresswellian remains are most readily found. The main food of these people appears to have been wild horses.

Gough's Cave contains definite burials of these late Upper Palaeolithic people: of at least three adults and two children. There are signs of defleshing of the bodies with flint knives and even cooking, so cannibalism again suggests itself. But the bones were carefully deposited in the cave in a way that suggests ritualistic, ideological procedures. Promising researches are afoot to investigate the DNA traces preserved on these bones: already there is evidence for a real continuity of descent from these late Upper Palaeolithic people right down to our own times.

A number of rather hard-to-see wall engravings of animals have been identified recently at the Cresswell Crags and British caves do furnish instances of portable artistic productions: abstract designs from Gough's Cave as well as several of the Cresswell locations. Church Hole at Cresswell has turned up a notched bone pendant as well as those engravings and a rather stylish horse's head sketch on an animal rib fragment was found in Robin Hood's Cave dating to about 12,500 BP. This was late in the day for all such Upper Paleolithic art: the finest cave art of France and Spain, for example in the form of the wonderful paintings found in cave systems at Altamira (Spain) and Lascaux (France), dates to between 20,000 and

15,000 BP during the Magdalenian phase of the Upper Palaeolithic. The late Magdalenian people made much of bone and antler in their technological as well as artistic output, along with smaller blade tools of flint that point towards the microlithic developments of postglacial times.

The End of the Ice Age

Just before the end of the ice age, a climate down-turn at around 11,000 BP signalled the end of the Upper Palaeolithic in Britain, when people were probably forced back across the land-bridge into continental Europe. There followed a series of warmer and colder fluctuations as the ice age came quite rapidly to an end and the erstwhile game-rich landscape grew wooded again. Sea levels rose as the glaciers retreated and melted, though Britain was not to be finally separated from continental Europe until about 8,500 years ago. By that time a warmer, moister, more wooded world had spread over Europe, where hunters with little or no use for caves built wooden huts and boats, hunting and fishing with a new technology of tiny bladelets (obviously mounted in composite tools and weapons with wooden handles) and elaborate hooks, snares and traps. The bow and arrow had been widely adopted in about 13,000 BP (though its origins may go back a long way further in Africa) and was used with advantage by the last of the late Upper Palaeolithic people who pursued the retreating reindeer into areas of northern Europe where neither beasts nor men had been able to venture during the ice age. (These reindeer hunters may have been taking the first steps towards organized herding, an idea which would lead on in time to the domestication of animals in the farming revolution.) For all that it was much warmer, the postglacial world was often less rich in easily accessed game supplies and life became harder in some ways. The outstanding artistic productivity of the ice age hunters disappeared with them and the end of their way of life, and painted pebbles and rather rudimentary sketching on bones took the place of glorious polychrome pictures on cave walls.

In some places, where perhaps seafood was easily come by, settled living was inaugurated in a way never quite possible before, even in the well-frequented caves of

Neanderthal and Crô-Magnon times. Settled living, the domestication of animals and the cultivation of plants would bring about a revolution indeed in human affairs: there would be villages, towns, cities, social hierarchies and class divisions, food surpluses and bureaucracies to administer them with written records; worst of all, there would be drudgery. All the panoply of civilization was in place in the Near East by about 5,500 BP, though not yet in the Eurasian heartland of the Neanderthal and Crô-Magnon folk, who epitomize the idea of living in caves. Of course, in various places people went on living in caves or burying their dead in caves (as they do here and there to this day) but the progress of human technology in step with climate change had put an end to the 'cave man' era and the way of life that went with it. While it lasted (and it was a very long time) that era produced much to astonish and impress us and even more to make us ponder the processes by which full humanity evolved in the world.